The Spirit of the Sloth

Exposing & Escaping Procrastination and Idleness

MAE P. GAFFNEY

The Spirit of the Sloth: Exposing & Escaping Procrastination and Idleness

Published in the United States of America

Scripture unless otherwise indicated taken from the Holy Bible, NEW INTERNATIONAL VERSION/NIV.

ISBN-13: 978-1983884115

ISBN-10: 1983884111

DEDICATION

This book is dedicated to my daughter, Tykeysha, who next to the Lord holds the most cherished and valuable part of my heart. You are truly a great daughter. Thank you for your kindness and your assistance in publishing this book.

To my Pastor, and spiritual father LoEarl Flowers. Thank you for the prayers, words of impartation and motivation.

&

In memory of my dearest and best friends Hazel E. Palmer and Glory J. Rivers. Your friendship is forever cherished.

CONTENTS

THE SPIRIT OF THE SLOTH

ACKNOWLEDGMENTS

A special thanks to Joyce Jones, Craig Mims, Maverick Singleton, Rodrick Caldwell, and Eddie Pugh, Sr., who each shared with me dreams and visions that were given to them about my writing a book. Your dreams pushed me forward.

To Jay Pettaway, Joseph Palmer Jr., Alvin Rhodes, James Moorer, Debbie Campbell, Deborah Johnson, Angeline Taylor, Thelma Pressley, Craig Mims, Betty Byrd, Mellan Johnson, and my sister Jennifer Parmer for your continued support, encouragement and motivation.

To Renee Taylor for your unconditional friendship, and laboring with me in prayer and warfare.

Most importantly, I offer my sincere thankfulness to the Almighty God for his love and favor. I thank Him for the divine revelation of the Word through the guidance of the Holy Spirit during this great task.

INTRODUCTION

Have you ever been in a place in your life where you had tasks to complete, and you really thought you had it altogether? You believed that you were moving forward and getting things done. However, when you looked around, you realized that nothing had been completed. Did you immediately start to make excuses for yourself? Perhaps you decide to take a nap. After the nap, you decided that the task could wait until tomorrow. Tomorrow turned into the next tomorrow, and the tomorrow after that.

After all the tomorrows had come and gone, the willingness and the motivation to complete the task had suddenly gone with it. However, the fact that you did not complete the task, seemed not to bother you as much as you had assumed it would, so you decide to move ahead and create an entirely new set of tasks, although the first set of tasks were never completed.. Much like the initial task, you end up putting the next set of tasks off into your "land of tomorrow" and

nothing ever gets done. Laziness, is what initially comes to mind…
however technically speaking we are operating in the spirit of the
sloth.

The scripture lets us know that God does not want us to have the
spirit of *the* sloth because we will get nothing. **(Proverb 13:4 The
soul of the sluggard desireth, and hath nothing: but the soul of
the diligent shall be made fat).** God wants us to produce and have
abundantly.

This spirit is sometimes an innate and lingering part of us that
facilitates procrastination, results in low productivity and ultimately
creates a life of few if any real accomplishments. If we were to take
the animal, the mammal, the sloth into consideration. This spirit has
us, like this animal, spending much of our time sleeping and eating.
Oh…and breeding. The sloth does not work to build a nest for
himself. Instead he finds a leafy area and simply falls asleep, hanging
completely upside down. Yes. The sloth is lazy. He spends almost
every waking moment (although there are very few of them), quietly
munching on leaves with little time for grooming or any other

activities. Do you know of a person with these behaviors? Are you this person?

While writing this book, God revealed to me that I too had been giving place for the spirit of the sloth to operate. This book blessed me to understand that procrastination hinders us from reaching our goals and experiencing the often timely blessings that God has in store for us.

As you read this book you will see areas in your life in which you have allowed this spirit to flow and discover ways to overcome this spirit.

1

THE SPIRIT OF THE SLOTH

My mornings begin with prayer. I would set my alarm for 5:00 am daily to ensure that I get this done before all else. Good for me, right? However, in addition to prayer, was my daily "to-do" tasks. Nevertheless, I would always find myself getting up for prayer and then going back to sleep... waking up to read scriptures... then back to sleep again. Look at the things that I had scribbled down as part of my "to-do" tasks, ponder over those things that I had not written down, but knew needed to be done, found a reason not to do them, or became "busy" doing everything "except" for the tasks at hand and finally at the end of the day, realized that I had produced nothing.

Now, having a day or two when you need take a mental break or rest is perfectly okay. However, when your breaks become chronic (you break excessively and they interfere with your ability to produce) you have entered into the spirit of slothfulness.

One morning as I was praying and praising God, giving Him glory, thanking Him for being such an amazing God, a great God, a powerful God, a righteous God, a way out of no way God, the all-knowing God, I heard the Holy Spirit speak to me saying "You are carrying the spirit of the *Sloth!* "And in order for you to finish the tasks that are giving to you, the spirit of slothfulness must go.

The spirit of the sloth is an inward spirit of laziness. This slothful spirit can also cause one to adopt spirits of unwillingness, become unproductive, experience bouts of depression, lose motivation, and become comfortable with procrastination. A slothful spirit hinders one from being fruitful, productive and willing to carry out the plan of the Almighty God. Consequently, when the plan of God is not carried out it can keep the promises of God from being released in our lives.

In the Gospel of Matthew, the parable of the talents (***Matthew25:14-***

28, KJV).; verse 15 points out that God already knows our abilities and if we believe and trust Him and are willing to utilize what we have been given, we are destined to become Kingdom Builders.

As found in the KJV of the Holy Bible, *(Matthew 25:14 -28):*

For the kingdom of heaven is as a man travelling into a far country, who called his own servants, and delivered unto them his goods.

15 And unto one he gave five talents, to another two, and to another one; to every man according to his several ability; and straightway took his journey.

16 Then he that had received the five talents went and traded with the same, and made them other five talents.

17 And likewise he that had received two, he also gained other two.

18 But he that had received one went and digged in the earth, and hid his lord's money.

19 After a long time the lord of those servants cometh, and reckoneth with them.

20 And so he that had received five talents came and brought other five talents, saying, Lord, thou deliveredst unto me five talents: behold, I have gained beside them five talents more.

21 His lord said unto him, Well done, thou good and faithful servant: thou hast been faithful over a few things, I will make thee ruler over many things: enter thou into the joy of thy lord.

22 He also that had received two talents came and said, Lord, thou deliveredst unto me two talents: behold, I have gained two other talents beside them.

23 His lord said unto him, Well done, good and faithful servant; thou hast been faithful over a few things, I will make thee ruler over many things: enter thou into the joy of thy lord.

24 Then he which had received the one talent came and said, Lord, I knew thee that thou art an hard man, reaping where thou hast not sown, and gathering where thou hast not strawed:

25 And I was afraid, and went and hid thy talent in the earth: lo, there thou hast that is thine.

26 His lord answered and said unto him, Thou wicked and slothful servant, thou knewest that I reap where I sowed not, and gather where I have not strawed:

27 Thou oughtest therefore to have put my money to the

exchangers, and then at my coming I should have received

mine own with usury.

28 Take therefore the talent from him, and give it unto him

which hath ten talent.

Verse 15 is implication that productivity is a result of using our God given abilities expeditiously. The word of God is letting us know *(vs. 16-23)* if we are not lazy and is willing to do the call of God he promise he will make us rulers over much and that the joy of the Lord is ours. Therefore we understand that that spirit of slothfulness, which brings about procrastination, lack or productivity and even depression is certainly not of God.

Additionally, giving place to a slothful spirit can cause one to operate in the spirits of: excuses, assuming and fear *(vs. 24 & 25)*. The main goal of these spirits is to keep us from producing. The enemy knows if he keeps us *slothful* and *lazy*, there will be no *productivity*. And where there is no productivity there is no fruit. God requires us to bear much fruit. This is referenced by **John 15:8** (KJV) of the Holy Bible:

Herein is my Father glorified, that ye bear much fruit; so shall ye be my disciples.

A slothful spirit can degrade ones ability and standards to "wickedness and laziness *"(vs. 26-28)* this spirit can also cause ones blessings to be given to someone else. Yes I know we have all lived by the saying that "what God got for me it is for me." We have been taught this. However, we fail to realize that there are certain principles that we must follow in order to have the true blessings of God released to us. Of course, blessings come in many forms. But my question to you is if we know that God wants us to "prosper and be in good health… even as our souls prospers", if He wants us to have "life and life more abundantly", if He promises to "satisfy us with long life" why are not more of us reaping the blessings of his promises? God is not like man, therefore He cannot lie. Could we be in fact limiting ourselves from receiving the fullness of His promises because we have not yet learned to activate those principles that unlock the blessings of Heaven? Could our failure to relinquish laziness and the slothful spirit be a key factor in what is preventing us from experiencing true Kingdom living? Yes, Yes, and Yes!

Many of us have not unlocked our true blessings because we have been too lazy to recognize the abilities and talents that God has given to us. Others of us have recognized our abilities and talents, but are either too lazy to put work behind our faith or too complacent to allow faith to lead us to our next level of Kingdom living.

Let us take for an example, members of the Grapefruit Club. In this example, Ms. Peanut is the one responsible for picking up the grapefruits and making sure that they are at the meeting every Tuesday night by 7:00 PM. Nevertheless, and without fail, Ms. Peanut is never prepared on Tuesday nights with the grapefruits. She sleeps most of the day, she sits around on the couch for several hours watching television or simply wondering off into random thoughts. With a few minutes remaining before meeting time, she remembers that she is low on gas and needs to go to the gas station. For some reason, she has developed a sweet tooth and decides to stop by the drive-thru for an ice cream sundae. When she finally arrives at the

meeting, it is almost over. The other club members are upset

because there was no grapefruit… as usual. Her excuse to the group

was that she was busy all day and that bringing the grapefruit added

too much to her already outrageous "to-do" list.

There are a few things going on with Ms. Peanut. Although there

could be other factors in her life that prevent her from her full level

of effectiveness. But as it pertains to the task at hand, we can see how

the spirit of slothfulness hindered productivity. This spirit not only

effected Ms. Peanut but caused the members of the group to also feel

the consequences of the spirit of the sloth.

The Bible tells us that the spirit of slothfulness will

have us so lazy that the mind believes that eating is

too much work. **(Proverbs 19:24 KJV) A slothful**

man hideth his hand in his bosom, and will not so

much as bring it to his mouth again. Let us add

(Proverbs 26:15) The slothful hideth his hand in

his bosom; it grieveth him to bring it again to his mouth. One passage says (NIV) *the sluggard buries his hand in the dish; he is too lazy to bring it back to his mouth.*

The spirit of slothfulness is a weapon that the enemy will use against us *(which I will discuss in the next chapter)* to cause us to be unfruitful, lazy and unwilling to carry out the plan of God and it hinder us from receiving abundant blessings. It keeps us from enhancing the work of the Kingdom.

The spirit of the sloth can and will cause the mind to be in bondage. It promotes the mind in to thinking*: **I know what to do, but I choose not to do.*** This spirit speaks and says to us: "don't move, don't get up, and don't show up on time". It plays a very big part in encouraging us not to be productive. The spirit of slothfulness births deception and this hinders us from inheriting the promises of God. **(Hebrews 6:12 KJV)** (*That ye be not slothful, but followers of them who through faith and patience inherit the promises).*

We must be willing, obedient and ready to do the task that God have for us. We must follow instructions and submit to God's authority and not listen to the spirit of slothfulness. This spirit will think for us if we allow it to do so. This spirit is a mind binding strong-hold it can cause us not to trust the Almighty God. Slothfulness leads us to neglect duties and causes us to give up trying. It promotes fear and it brings us to a place of being un-concern about the things of God, others and ourselves. Slothfulness is a distraction and distractions can cause destruction.

The spirit of slothfulness prevents us from working. It feeds off of idleness and when the mind becomes idle it bring the spirit of worthless, laziness and excessiveness which birth depression. It is very important that we guard our minds with the Word of God at all times so that this spirit does not allow us to experience a false sense of overwhelm and exhaustion. Yes. Both exhaustion and overwhelm can indeed be "false" particularly if the spirit of the sloth is present. Have you ever felt tired, overwhelmed or exhausted for no physical or mental reason at all? Did this feeling result in your becoming unproductive but all the while "thinking" that you were getting something done?

We have *the ability* and *the authority* from *God* to be fruitful, to be productive. God is expecting us not to be lazy with the talents that he have entrusted us with therefor we must stay focused and be producers. Activeness and time is very important to God.

2

THE ENEMY'S WEAPONS

Slothfulness is indeed a weapon of the devil because it is said to be one of the seven deadly sins. Dorothy Sayers describes sloth as a " sin that believes in nothing, seeks to know nothing, find purpose in nothing, lives for nothing and [it]refuses the joy that comes from God."

The enemy uses it against us because it brings us in a place of inactivity and laziness. Being lazy not only prevents us from fully operating in the grace of God, but shows up in the way we move, live and interact with our family, friends and society as a whole. This spirit is a very powerful weapon because it can destroy lives, hope, destinies, marriages, ministries and more. It takes you into a consistent state of "delay", meaning that your reality is a collection of tasks that never get started, or if you start them, they are never completed.

The enemy uses slothfulness as a weapon of **neglect**. *(to pay no* *attention or little attention to what should be done*). When we are slothful and put things off it can cause problems. *(Ecclesiastes 10:18) By much slothfulness the building decayeth; and through idleness of the hands the house droppeth through)*. As you see, by much slothfulness and idleness, things are undone, and the house falls apart because of the weapon of neglect.

This weapon of slothfulness can destroy. Let's look how this weapon can be use by the enemy:

The enemy use slothfulness to destroy marriages.

The spirit of the sloth has ruined many marriages because it is a weapon that the enemy uses in marriage to promote selfishness. For example, it can have a couple operating in a spirit that renders them too lazy to think about or consider the other. This spirit facilitates the thoughts that one spouse should do something before or instead of the other, leading to a situation where nothing gets done for the household.

Take Mr. and Mrs. Jones for example: There is a book on the floor and someone needs to pick it up. The Jones' come home from a nice dinner. They both see that there is obviously a book on the floor. Mrs. Jones thinks about picking up the book but decides to get a drink a water and assumes that Mr. Jones will pick up the book. Mr. Jones assumed that Mrs. Jones would pick it up. After all, she is the wife and it is her responsibility to keep things nice and in order around the house, he thinks. *(they both have the ability to pick it up)*. The book stays on the floor for three days and neither one picks it up. Instead they each make excuses about why they could not pick up the book and quarrel over why the other should have picked up the book.. Now the enemy has used the poor innocent book, exaggerated by the spirit of slothfulness which introduced laziness on the part of both spouses and "unwillingness" for either of the spouses to accept responsibility or to apologize, as a reason to start chaos in the Jones' marriage.

Now because of the spirit of unwillingness of the Jones' it effects the intimacy in the marriage. Slothfulness is an ***intimacy*** destroyer, so now the spirit brings in the spirit of ***excuses***. Mrs.

23

Jones is tired and unwilling to show affection to Mr. Jones and Mr. Jones is feeling neglected and unwanted. Now they waste time not communicating. And when they decide to communicate they both bring up old issues, or even the poor blameless book and allow the enemy to cause problems in their marriage. We must recognize this weapon is aiming to take away unity so it can destroy the strength of the marriage. Marriage requires sacrifice not laziness.

The spirit of the sloth is a weapon to hinder hope and destiny.

The enemy knows if we lose hope our destiny will be destroyed. We cannot afford to be slothful in our hope, because hope is expectation of what we believe in by faith for our destiny.

If we are too lazy to hold on to our expectations, destiny will be destroyed. Slothfulness keeps us from a healthy prayer life and this can rob us from our destiny and it will hinder us from getting to the place where God had for us.

A weapon to bind the mind

This weapon uses the mind. Its goal is to make us think that we cannot press forward, we cannot accomplish anything, and we do not have the energy to do anything. We must recognize that this is a spirit that the enemy has attached to our lives and it will destroy us.

Slothfulness is a very powerful weapon, and it releases the ammunition of despair, depression, heaviness, restlessness, idleness and this lead to the road of destruction. Slothfulness is a very dangerous weapon it is a killer, it breeds disappointment and disappointment breeds hopelessness, hopelessness breeds depression and depression rob us of our motivation.

The enemy knows when we lose our motivation it hinders the mind and when our mind is hindered we do not have the will power to work nor carry out the plans of God. Remember this spirit gives excuses. *(Proverbs 26:13 KJV): The slothful man saith, There is a lion in the way; a lion is in the streets.* With this, we hold to the excuse that it is someone else's fault that we are not producing. "Someone else" is in the way. "Something" else is in the way that makes us unable to do what we are supposed to be doing. "I would have finished my assignment but my dog was barking"… "I would have been on time but my sister is still here"… We are not producing because we are slothful and are not applying the ability that God have instilled in us.

Slothfulness will take resident in our mind and this will cause us not to be active. It produces nothing positive. It can cause the natural and spiritual eye to see opportunity, work and advancements as fear and discomfort. And when fear is in operation doubt is present also. Fear is a spirit of intimidation given by the enemy*. (II Timothy 1:7 For God hath not given us the spirit of fear; but of power, and of love, and of a sound mind.).* Fear will intimidate us and cause us not to go forward. For example, I personally wasted time for many years wrestling with this spirit and making lazy excuses for not being productive. And yes I became slothful and blamed others for my not fulfilling the plans of God.

I allowed the spirit of the sloth to cause me to become un-focused, uncreative, un- motivated, and this hindered me from the promises of God. The Word of God reminded me that because man was created in God's image, man was not designed to be slothful. God, from the beginning of the Word, worked. He was not lazy. He was creating the World. *(Genesis 1:1 KJV)In the beginning God created the heaven and the earth.*

Look at: **Genesis 1:27-28 (So God created man in his own image, in the image of God created he him; male and female created he them. 28. And God blessed them, and God said unto them, Be fruitful, and multiply, and replenish the earth, and subdue it: and have dominion over the fish of the sea, and over the fowl of the air, and over every living thing that moveth upon the earth**.)

Here we see that after God created man and woman, and blessed them He gave His first spoken command to them: *do something*, *work*, *produce* society and *manage* the creation. We cannot allow this weapon to deter us from what God have commanded us to do. Slothfulness and fear together is so powerful it can exhaust the mind and body and this will cause us not to be able to stand in faith. Slothfulness is a dangerous weapon. One of its missions is to hit the mind and cause us to believe that we do not have to be producers. While faith the size of the mustard seed is all the faith we need, we must work in order for faith to perform the job it was designed to perform.

(Faith without works is dead) James 2:14

Faith wants a job. Faith does not want to be slothful and lying around doing nothing. As a matter of fact, faith does not want a break, and it does not ask for a vacation.

3

SYMPTOMS OF THE SLOTHFUL

We know by now that slothfulness is one of the enemy's greatest and most powerful spirits. It is used against us to hinder God's plan and to hold us back from the blessings that God has in store for us.

Some of the symptoms of slothfulness are denial, excuses, procrastination, and unwillingness. The Webster's Dictionary defines a symptom as something that indicates the existence of something and serving as evidence of it. Perhaps you have recognized some of these symptoms in your life but did not understand the true essence of the sloth.

We must recognize and admit these symptoms so we can move forward and be fruit- bearers so we can be helpers in building of the Kingdom of God. Keep in mind from the previous chapters that God desires productiveness. So we must not be lazy we have to study and know that God want us to be aware of the devil devices.

The Apostle Paul was not slothful nor in denial of the tricks of Satan. He was well aware and kept a willing mind to stay battle ready. We cannot be lazy. We are at war. Being slothful will destroy us. The scripture says to us :(**II Corinthians 2:11 KJV Lest Satan should get an advantage of us: for we are not ignorant of his devices.)** We must understand the devil's tricks and traps. Let us examine how *slothful* symptoms can begin.

<u>Excuses:</u>

We find ourselves constantly making excuses or saying that there is not enough time to do the things that needed to have been done but we know within ourselves we have wasted time doing nothing. Making excuses for our inactiveness and feeling fearful of something always being in our way, allowing excuses to hinder us from being productive. **(Proverbs 22:3)**. The sloth spirit helped us to invent reasons and create excuses to neglect responsibilities.

The enemy always gives excuses: *I would have done it, I could have done it, I would have been there,* **but!** **Making an effort is better than a good excuse.**

Being Unprepared:

We are slothful and believe that we should not prepare for each season or for anything because we are too lazy to work. *(Proverbs 6:6-8)* .when there is an unprepared spirit the person always waits for someone else to tell him/her to work. They have no mind to work or to prepare for anything in life. We must not allow the spirit of the sloth to cause us to be lazy and unprepared for the coming of the Lord. The Gospel of Matthew informs us *(Matthew 25-1-13)* to be prepared and be ready. So this let us know that we must be ready not getting ready.

Love Idle Companionship

Apostle Paul tell us *(II Thessalonians 3:10-14)* to avoid anyone that walks in idleness. If anyone is not willing to work let him not eat.. We must be aware of the company we keep. God does not use lazy idle people to carry out his tasks but the devil does. The devil likes it when we choose to associate with people who have idle minds. If we find that we love idle companionship (being in the company of lazy people) we are allowing an opportunity for the spirt of laziness to become a part of us.

Enjoys Excessive Sleeping.

(Proverbs 19:15) The spirit of the sloth causes deep sleep to fall upon us. This person is generally sleepy at all times and indulges themselves in it.

This spirit causes one to sleep day and night and because it is a lazy spirit it has no concern for God, work, others or self. We need to be very alert because the enemy will have us sleeping when we should be working, or studying the word of God. Excessive sleeping, particularly without a known physical, mental, or medical cause, will produce laziness and laziness will produce excessive sleep.

Procrastinating:

Procrastination is the act of willfully delaying the doing of something that should be done. If we are not careful it will become a habitual way of handling any task. Procrastination is the result of being lazy. We have allowed the spirit of procrastinating to hinder us from sharing the gospel with the lost. *(Luke 14:21)* Jesus wants us to *"Go out quickly"* but we delay in making the call.

Procrastinating spirits love tardiness, do not like starting on time, know what should be done today but put it off for tomorrow and is not concern about completing a task on time. This spirit also promotes unsoundness. It plays with our mind so we can become double minded. And the bible declares that a double minded man is unstable in all he does *(James 1:8 L.B)*

Procrastination leads us to "put off 'til tomorrow what we could and should do today". It's primary communication is *"not now, tomorrow, just wait, I got time, I will be there when I get there, I will get to it* or *I was going to do it but….".*

Procrastination can also be a by-product of indecisiveness.   A procrastinating slothful person wants much but he gets little. *(Proverbs 13:4)* because he is unwilling and too lazy to asked God for help.   He maintains stronghold symptoms such as being unwilling to motivate himself to change, and he holds on to *lateness* and *tardiness* as a valuable gift. This symptom can hide itself because we have a tendency to practice it for so long that it becomes to be accepted as a way of living.

Not Attending Church.

This is one of the slothful symptoms that the enemy has used to deceive the body of Christ. The devil has made us believe that attending church is not important and being on time for service does not matter. If we do not attend church we are against the Word of God. *(Hebrews 10:25 KJV)   Not forsaking the assembling of ourselves together, as the manner of some is; but exhorting one*
another: and so much the more, as ye see the day approaching).

Slothful members' symptoms are very visible. They will find excuses not to attend church. For example, if church service is on Sunday, the enemy will start on Friday, Saturday and early Sunday morning working to invent reasons that seem justifiable for missing church. Oversleeping, being tired, feeling too ill to get dressed… just in time for service is a true symptom that this symptom is evident in our lives. We are allowing the enemy to keep us from fellowshipping and from hearing a word from God. When we are in a spirit of not wanting to attend church, this is not the spirit of the Almighty God.

No matter what kind of excuse the devil makes up for us it is not acceptable to God. We are responsible to study to show ourselves approve to God.. We cannot continue to be lazy and not do what God has instructed us according to His Word to do. We must study the word of God; slothfulness is not a right spirit. Not attending church is not acceptable. When we constantly make excuses that there is not enough time to do the things that needed to have been done but we know within ourselves we have wasted time doing nothing. When we become slothful and do not attend church the spirit of the sloth causes us not to feel connected to the body of Christ and when we feel this way it promotes a spirit of selfishness. When we are selfish we will become slothful in *giving*, slothful in *serving*, slothful in *being on time for service*, just slothful in helping in any areas of the ministry.

We must beware of our selfish and slothful ways. ***Haggai 1:5-14 NIV*** reminds us that we can have lazy and selfish spirits when it comes to the house of God, the writer say this is what the Lord Almighty says: ***"Give careful thought to your ways***. Because of the sloth spirit things become all about us. Thank God, for a loving God that will point out that this spirit is operating in us. Our selfish and slothful ways can hinder us from blessing the house of God.

Having Someone Else Do Your Job

How many of us can admit to this symptom? We are lazy and have been passing our tasks along to someone else. Not in the spirit of delegation, or because we could not do it… but because we are too lazy to do it.

Too Lazy To Go To Bed.. Or To the Bathroom

We want to get up and go to bed but we are lazy and will not apply the energy to get up off of the couch.   Or worse, having to use the bathroom in the middle of the night. But the bathroom seems so far away! So, you just hold it and go back to sleep. Does this sound like you? There are other symptoms that the Holy Ghost will reveal to us to let us know that the spirit of slothfulness has become a part of our lives, and because of this spirit we have been unproductive and have missed out on or ultimately delayed the plan of God. If we do not start working to remedy and cure our symptoms, they will escalate into serious problems.

4

A SPIRITUAL SLOTH ATTACKS

What Is A Spiritual Attack?

A spiritual attack is a series of events coordinated by the demonic realm in order to terminate the promises of God. Its plan is to shipwreck faith, oppress our mind and destroy our destiny.

Paul reminds us *"lest Satan should take advantage of us for we are not ignorant of his devices." (11 Corinthians 2:11)*. We cannot be slothful in studying and knowing the Word of God. The scripture is letting us know that we shouldn't be ignorant of Satan tricks but if we are too lazy to know the word the devil will take advantage of us. He has been studying our thoughts, our action and behavior since the beginning of time. He used the spirit of slothfulness to hinder our success. He used slothfulness to keep us from holding on to the Word so he can attack our faith. He hates faith which the Word produces. *(Roman 10:17)*.

We must keep our spiritual eye open and know when the sloth attack is upon us. With our spiritual eye we can see his attacks. His attacks make us slothful in lack of **_spiritual passion:_** which come to steal our desires for the thangs of God, it makes us lazy in our *prayer life, bible studying, fasting,* and *witnessing.*

He attacks us with **_frustration:_** which comes to discourage us so we can quit our assignments. Frustration also brings *stress, sadness,* and it will get us to the point of losing hope and faith of the promises of God. Frustration is weightiness and the bible tell us to lay aside every weight, and the sin which doth so easily beset us. *(Hebrews 12: 1)*

The sloth attacks us with **_sluggishness_** or **_tiredness_** we are under spiritual attacks when we are feeling tired and that tiredness separates us from doing the things God has called us to do.

The sloth attacks us with **_inactiveness_** because he knows that there are times we are to slothful to move and this causes us not to participate in the work of the ministry.

The sloth spirit attacks us in *giving*, which make us stingy to the house of the Lord. The easy way to invite devourers and poverty into our life is to be lazy and slack in giving to God *(Proverbs 10:4)* *He becometh poor that dealeth with slack hand: but the hand of diligent maketh rich.*

(Proverbs 28:22 ESV) A stingy man hastens after wealth and does not know that poverty will come upon him.

The sloth spirit attacks our *worth*; tell us that we do not amount to anything. Tell us that we are failures and that we will never succeed. He weights us down with every mistake we have made so that he can lure us in to a place of slothfulness where we can be unproductive.

We need to stay alert and not worry about what the enemy thinks. God has a great end for us. *(Jeremiah 29:11),* *for I know the thoughts that I think toward you, Saith the LORD, thoughts of peace, and not of evil, to give you and expected end.*

5

DANGERS OF BEING SLOTHFUL

Slothfulness is not a friend it is and enemy to us. The Bible lets us know that it will cause problems and harm one way of another.

Slothfulness: leads to poverty *(Proverbs 6:6-11)*. Lazy people make no effort for physical things so they will not do it for emotional or spiritual rewards either.

Slothfulness: leads to shame: *(Proverbs 10:5).* Things that bring honor to a person come with effort. A slothful life caused by laziness brings shame on those who depend on them.

Slothfulness: leads to dissatisfaction *(Proverbs 13:4).* Ultimately slothfulness depletes joy. Allows us to become envious and leads to depression.

Slothfulness: leads to slavery *(Proverbs 12:24).* Slothful people still want things but become indebted to others. Lazy people can end up being poor financially, emotionally and spiritually.

Slothfulness: leads to excuses *(Proverbs 26:13-14)* A slothful person is an expert at making excuses; why things should be done tomorrow, why things are not finished, and always blames others for things they should have done. They think that someone else is in their way or is preventing them from doing more, doing better or doing what they have been assigned to do.

Slothfulness: lead to wastefulness *(Proverbs 18:9)* A slothful person wastes his time, energy, talent and opportunities by not doing nothing. Lazy peoples will waste other people's time as well, leading to more work to be done by the person who is not the lazy one.

Slothfulness: is a dangerous spirit. It loves inactiveness, excesses sleep, idleness, and entertainment more than work.

6

OVERCOMING SLOTHFULNESS

Well, what do I say about myself now? Do I say Lord I have been operating in the spirit of the sloth? I have been slothful. I have been avoiding physical and spiritual work. I knew what to do, when to do it. but I failed to do it. Now Lord, I am asking you how to remove this spirit from my life. I believe within my heart that *"I Am Better Than This."* I must conquer this spirit.

Suggested ways to overcome

First, we must recognize and admit that the spirit is at work within us. Do not patty cake around with it. Do not try to make excuses for it. Just call it what it is… laziness, idleness, slothfulness.. the exact terminology does not matter as long as you can identify and call out the spirit.

Conduct a self-assessment of your life. Identify what the enemy is using to cause your lack of concern and what is hindering you from being motivated and taking action to do those things that you are supposed to be doing. Remember that it is written in the Word of God, that we should not be ignorant of Satan's devices *(II Corinthians 2:11).* We are at war! The devil hates us and he wants us to be slothful and unproductive so we must be aware of his tools, tricks and traps.

If the enemy is using the spirit of being *tired* then you must sacrifice some time for rest. If he is using the spirit of being *afraid,* you must ask yourself what are you afraid of? This is the task that you should be doing. Why are you afraid? You have great potential. You have a goals you need to reach.

We can also remind ourselves of the Word and its assurance that greater is within us: *(1John 4:4)* and God has not given us a spirit of fear *(1Timothy 1:7).* These verses from the holy Word let us know that we can overcome any hindrance in our lives. Now is the time that we must start commanding fear to go in the name of Jesus. We can take authority over our tasks. Speak with boldness and say, " *I will do this, and fear must go.*" Walk in the power of faith and not fear.

Slothfulness causes us to lose inspiration and motivation. Becoming organized and prioritizing tasks will help to facilitate the tasks with more ease. We have to free our minds as well as our physical environments from the clutter. Get rid of tasks that are not driving us forward and focus on those that will be necessary in order for us to accomplish the mission at hand. We must get rid of lazy thinking and lazy sayings such as: *"Lord I am so lazy today, 'I feel so worthless, 'Lord I'm not worth a nickel, why me? I will try to do the best that I can, I can't, what if?"Proverbs 18:21- Death and life are in the power of the tongue...* Words can hinder us from overcoming the spirit of the sloth.

When you recognize that you are not performing up to your best, *stop! Use the weapon of prayer* and this will help you to move and be motivated toward our task. Speak positive and motivating words: *It is time to go forward, it time to move, it is time for a shift, it is time to accomplish my goal, I can do all things through Christ that strengthens me, I am better than this.*

Sometimes we spend time worrying about the past. This can cause us to be in a slothful spirit and prevents us from embracing the present. Being in distress about past issues can and will produce the spirit of slothfulness. Dwelling on the mistakes of the past and failing to move forward according to God's timeline is not pleasing to God.

Let the devil know that you are going to start this day and will finish the tasks at hand. We often lose our will-power to perform and the enemy knows that if there is no will-power there is no motivation. We must pray and press until we get the victory. To over-come this spirit we must put our faith to work. Faith demands to be employed. (*James 2:14*). Faith without work is dead. We must change our thinking. We must believe that the spirit of the sloth will not control us anymore because we are better than that! We will overcome this spirit because we are going to: pray, admit that it is operating, we are going to get organize, we are going to set our priority in order, we are going to be motivated, we are going to get rid of distractions, we are going to watch what we say, we are going to fight the spirit of procrastination, we will produce will-power, we will have energy and we will have faith because we are going to stand on the word of God and believe that we are more than conquerors *(Romans 8:37)* through Him who loved us. We know that we can be victorious over this spirit. The scripture uses the phrase , _MORE THAN_, which means we will not only achieve victory, but we are exceedingly victorious.

(I believe it is appropriate right now: to take a pause and tell God thank you).

Satan is our adversary and he uses the spirit of slothfulness to keep us from being that powerful productive successful vessel that God has chosen to complete an assignment. The devil will make the assignment appear as a giant before us because he knows this will cause fear and doubt to come in. Fear feeds procrastination, which we have identified to be a vice of slothfulness. We must remember that we are not alone; *Jesus* has empowered us to be winners.

God loves us and he wants the best for us. I just believe that He intended for us to excel and prosper in life. *(3 John 1:2).* We are His children. We were created to be successful. We were created to live as Kingdom children, because our father is THE KING. If you consider living in the castle with the King as his children. His children want for nothing. They eat the best, they wear the best, they live the best, they are privy to the best services, they feel protected, they walk in their inheritance. It is their very birth right to enjoy the benefits of being a child of the King. The same applies to us as God's children. Knowing that we are His children gives us the right to let go of the spirit of slothfulness so the we can reap the benefits of our inheritance at every level.

We must examine ourselves, shut every door, and close every window and seal every crack in our lives that the enemy has placed to enter in. Stand on the word in: (*Ephesians 4:27)* that Apostle Paul writes to us" Neither give "place to the devil. The word "*place*" is the Greek word means *topos* , it refers to a specific, marked off geographical location it carries the idea of a *territory, region, zone* or *geographical* position it is from this word that we get the word for *topographical* map. Because the word *topos* depicts geographical location, this lets us know that the devil is after every region and zone of our lives: money, health, marriage, relationships employment, ministry, our mind and our will-power. He is so territorial he wants it all. We must fight to overcome the spirit of the sloth. We must keep our minds and spirits guarded with prayer and with the word of God. We can overcome this spirit. Jesus has anointed us with the power of the Holy Ghost. Our prayers are weapons against the enemy. We have the authority over the devil *(Luke 10:19-*

Behold, I give unto you power to tread on serpents and scorpions, and over all the power of the enemy: and nothing shall by any means hurt you).

To overcome the spirit of the sloth, we must apply and practice *diligence*. *(Careful, attention, persistent, endeavor. A diligent person is described as 'assiduous, thorough, not idle, not negligent, and not lazy).* When we are diligent we are self-discipline and self-discipline promotes goals, visions, and accountability.

Jesus tells us *(Matthew 24:46)* that *"Blessed is the servant whom his master, when he comes, will find so doing' – and*

not caught in idleness. Jesus expects responsibility, reliability and thoroughness from us. To overcome the spirit of the sloth, we must diligently yield our lives to God. And we must maintain a personal relationship with Him. ***Time*** is very important to God and we must use our energy to take advantage of what we have at the moment. When we spend time on past failures and past hurts it robs us of our ability to produce and complete tasks successfully.

7

MAINTAINING YOUR DELIVERANCE

The bible tells us *(Luke 11:24-26)* that when an evil spirit comes out of a person it searches for another person to reside in and if the evil spirit is unable to find someone else it goes back to the person it came out of. If the evil spirit returns and finds that person empty, it brings more evil spirits with it, making this person worse than before. If we want to maintain our deliverance from the spirit of the sloth we cannot allow ourselves to be idle- minded and empty of the Word of God.

This evil spirit can only return if we have allowed ourselves to be empty because we have been slothful in studying God's Word and in prayer. We must yield our freed areas to the infilling of the Holy Spirit and when we do this there is no room for the spirit of the Sloth to return.

We must see ourselves free from this spirit before we can become totally free. The Bible tells us to speak those things that are not as though they were. We can bring promises from the spiritual realm to the natural by calling those things that are not. *(Romans 4:17)*. We have to see ourselves coming out, being out and we must speak boldly in the atmosphere and declare and decree that we will not go back to the spirit of being slothful this will help us to maintain our deliverance. We cannot afford to sit around being lazy and not studying and meditating on God's Word.

The Holy Scriptures should be in our minds for meditation not just one day but every day. *Joshua 1:8 says; This book of the law shall not depart from your mouth, but shall meditate on it day and night, so that you may be careful to do according to all that is written in it, for then you will make your way prosperous, and then you will have success).* To maintain our deliverance, it is very important that we keep the Word of God upon our lips, in our hearts and on our minds.

My late church mother sang a song with the lyrics, *"there's a war going on and you better fight."* I found this song to be true because we are at war with this spirit and if we are going to maintain our deliverance from it, we must be battle ready and clothed with the Armor of God *(Ephesians 6:10-18).*

Be On Alert For These Two Old Habits: Procrastination & Excuses

Procrastination, as we learned from previous chapters is to put off intentionally the doing of something that should be done. There is no value in procrastinating it will manifests ***postponement***. This spirit is our enemy. If we are planning on getting our tasks done we must stay delivered and not allow this old habit to come back to reside within us.

In the book of II Corinthians 8:10-12; we notice that Paul does his best to encourage the congregation at Corinth to stop procrastinating *II Corinthians 8:10-12, And in this I give advice: it is to your advantage not only to be doing what you began and were desiring to do a year ago; but now you also must complete the doing of it; that as there was a readiness to desire it, so there also may be a completion out of what you have. (12 vs) for if there is first a willing mind, it is accepted according to what ones has, and not according to what he does not have.*

Paul was referring to their taking up a collection for their brethren. They had promised to do it a year ago and they still had not done it. Paul then encourages them to stop procrastinating and complete the task that they had started. *Take a look at verse 12*, it is suggested that there first must be a willing mind to finish the task. When our minds are willing, we are more likely to be motivated, and have a positive attitude toward getting the task done.

Beware of Making Excuses

We cannot go back to the lazy habit of making excuses. An excuse according to the Webster's Dictionary is to make allowance for short coming to serve as justification; to vindicate. There is no productivity in making excuses. If we do not stay delivered from the spirit of excuses it can hinder our Kingdom assignment. Take Moses for example:

Excuse #1. I cannot go unto Pharaoh and bring the children of Israel out of Egypt.

(Exodus 3:11 And Moses said unto God, Who am I, that I should go unto Pharaoh, and that I should bring forth the children of Israel out of Egypt?).

However, God let him know his excuse was not acceptable. God confirms to Moses that He would go with him and that He would give him the Promised Land.

(Exodus 3:12 And he said, Certainly I will be with thee; and this shall be a token unto thee, that I have sent thee: When thou hast brought forth the people out of Egypt, ye shall serve God upon this mountain)

Excuse #2. I do not want the people mad at me. Who should I say sent me?

(Exodus 3:13 And Moses said unto God, Behold, when I come unto the children of Israel, and shall say unto them, The God of your fathers hath sent me unto you; and they shall say to me, What is his name? what shall I say unto them?).

God again re-assures Moses that He has his back. In other words, God tells Moses, "You need not worry, because they know who I am".

(Exodus 3:14-15 And God said unto Moses, I AM THAT I AM: and he said, Thus shalt thou say unto the children of Israel, I AM hath sent me unto you.

15 And God said moreover unto Moses, Thus shalt thou say unto the children of Israel, The LORD God of your fathers, the God of Abraham, the God of Isaac, and the God of Jacob, hath sent me unto you: this is my name for ever, and this is my memorial unto all generations).

Excuse #3. What if they do not believe me?

(Exodus 4:1 And Moses answered and said, But, behold, they will not believe me, nor hearken unto my voice: for they will say, The LORD hath not appeared unto thee.)

God again offers reassurance and confirms it through the signs.

(Exodus 4:2-9- And the LORD said unto him, What is that in thine hand? And he said, A rod.

3 And he said, Cast it on the ground. And he cast it on the ground, and it became a serpent; and Moses fled from before it.

4 And the LORD said unto Moses, Put forth thine hand, and take it by the tail. And he put forth his hand, and caught it, and it became a rod in his hand:

5 That they may believe that the LORD God of their fathers, the God of Abraham, the God of Isaac, and the God of Jacob, hath appeared unto thee.

6 And the LORD said furthermore unto him, Put now thine hand into thy bosom. And he put his hand into his bosom: and when he took it out, behold, his hand was leprous as snow.

7 And he said, Put thine hand into thy bosom again. And he put his hand into his bosom again; and plucked it out of his bosom, and, behold, it was turned again as his other flesh.

8 And it shall come to pass, if they will not believe thee, neither hearken to the voice of the first sign, that they will believe the voice of the latter sign.9 And it shall come to pass, if they will not believe also these two signs, neither hearken unto thy voice, that thou shalt take of the water of the river, and pour it upon the dry land: and the water which thou takest out of the river shall become blood upon the dry land).

Excuse #4. Lord, " I, I, I, St-St –St-Stutter".

(Exodus 4:10 And Moses said unto the LORD, O my Lord, I am not eloquent, neither heretofore, nor since thou hast spoken unto thy servant: but I am slow of speech and of a slow tongue).

God again reassures Moses. God made Moses. He made his tongue. He would have the words for him to say.

(Exodus 4:11-12 And the LORD said unto him, Who hath made man's mouth? or who maketh the dumb, or deaf, or the seeing, or the blind? have not I the LORD?

12 Now therefore go, and I will be with thy mouth, and teach thee what thou shalt say).

<u>*Excuse #5.*</u> Well, I killed a man, I have been running for forty years. Can you find someone else for the task?

(Exodus 4:13 And he said, O my Lord, send, I pray thee, by the hand of him whom thou wilt send)

Again, despite Moses' many excuses, God reassures him that he is indeed the man for the task.

(Exodus 4:14-17And the anger of the LORD was kindled against Moses, and he said, Is not Aaron the Levite thy brother? I know that he can speak well. And also, behold, he cometh forth to meet thee: and when he seeth thee, he will be glad in his heart.

15 And thou shalt speak unto him, and put words in his mouth: and I will be with thy mouth, and with his mouth, and will teach you what ye shall do.

16 And he shall be thy spokesman unto the people: and he shall be, even he shall be to thee instead of a mouth, and thou shalt be to him instead of God.

17 And thou shalt take this rod in thine hand, wherewith thou shalt do signs).

When God has called us for a task he will not accept our excuses. We must be willing and obedient to the voice of God. To maintain our deliverance we cannot allow fear, laziness, unwillingness and intimidation to come back to be a part of our life.

We can maintain our deliverance from the spirit of the sloth, if we remember to:

Watch what we say (Proverbs 18:21)

Submit & Resist (James 4:7-8)

Study the Word of God (II Timothy 2:15)

Be both hearers and doers of the word

(James 1:22)

Put on the whole Armor of God

(Ephesians 6:11)

Know our enemy (I Peter 5:6-11)

Have a prayer life (Luke 18:1 & Isaiah 58)

Fill the empty space with the Word (Matthew12:43-45)

Walk in forgiveness (Matthew 6:14)

As we maintain our deliverance we must give God Glory and praise.

Through the Holy Spirit our great God has revealed to us this enemy;
the spirit of the sloth which we have found to be operating in
our lives and preventing us from reaping the full benefits of
Kingdom assignments.

We will stay focused, motivated, active and willing to do what is
given to us

to enhance kingdom work. We will not allow the weapons of
excuses,

procrastination and slothfulness to prosper. We will keep our
shield   and sword with us. We know that God has already given us
the

ability to accomplish whatever is set before us. *(Exodus 31:3*
And I

have filled him with the spirit of God, in wisdom, and in
understanding, and in knowledge, and in all manner of
workmanship).

8

SUGGESTED PRAYERS

Our Father In The Name of Jesus

I pray now that the atmosphere is conducive for deliverance from the devastating effects of the spirit of the sloth; Excuses, laziness, Inactiveness, idleness, deep sleep, slothfulness, unproductiveness, unwillingness, and procrastination,

We serve notice that your time is up. Lord forgive us, myself and any family members who may have opened doors that have ushered in its paralyzing effects.

We reverse the words of our mouths that have planted seeds of delay, defeat, disappointment, fear, and failure.

We call those seeds to come up, be unrooted and be destroyed that have kept us from healthy relationship, healthy business dealings, healthy financial ventures, kingdom building and spiritual wholeness.

We command that the plan and purposes of the enemy be replaced with Gods master plans.

We declare we see the end from the beginning and it is good

We declare we lack no more vision, imagination, creativity, intuition insight and foresight

We speak life over every dream that have been dormant and declare they are now being fulfilled

We like Abraham stagger not at the promises of God with unbelieve, but we declare we are strong in faith and give glory to God.

We bind and loose

According to your word Matthew 18:18 that declares whatsoever ye shall bind on earth shall be bound in heaven: and whatsoever ye shall loose on earth shall be loosed in heaven.

We bind…

We bind laziness

We bind inactiveness

We bind idleness

We bind deep sleep

We bind procrastination

We bind apathy

We bind heaviness

We bind dullness

We bind listlessness,

We bind excuses, in the name of Jesus

Now we loose…

Zeal

Readiness

Diligence

Hardworking

Lively

Freshness

Attentiveness

Willingness

Productivity

Successfulness, in the name of Jesus

I DECREE AND DECLARE THAT OUR SPIRTUAL MUSLCES BE RENEWED AND EVERY STIFF RIGID DEFORMED PART OF MY LIFE RECIVE RENEWED STRENGTH

We breathe life into the recesses of our mind and declare we now have the mind of Christ.

And are ready for every good work

Lead us

Guide us

Send us

Activate

Commission us

We declare we are now ready, able, motivated and available to do the will of God.

WE WILL NOT ACCEPT THE SPIRIT OF THE SLOTH NOMORE!!!!!!!

I DECREE AND DECLARE IN THE NAME OF JESUS THAT THE SPIRIT OF THE SLOTH MUST GO!!!!!!!!

9

SELF- ASSESSMENT

Rate Your Activities

(Your goal is to score 3 or less in each area. 1 is never or not at all, 5

is excessively.)

Currently, how often do you do the following:

Talk on the phone to avoid tasks	1 2 3 4 5
Scroll social media when you should be working	1 2 3 4 5
Turn off your alarm clock when you should get up	1 2 3 4 5
Spend hours watching TV when you have not completed your daily tasks	1 2 3 4 5
Take extra naps for no reason	1 2 3 4 5

Create new tasks in order to avoid completing the less desired tasks	1 2 3 4 5
Feel incompetent to complete tasks assigned to you, although you really are capable	1 2 3 4 5
Spend time being "busy" but producing little to no results	1 2 3 4 5
Spend time listening to others complain	1 2 3 4 5
Spend time with others who are unproductive	1 2 3 4 5

Don't Stress! Know Your Tasks!

Ask yourself the following questions. Do not allow slothfulness

to win.

What are your assignments?

Are you managing your time?

Are you procrastinating?

Are you setting goals?

Are you prioritizing?

Are you making a to-do list?

Are you enforcing punctuality?

Are you surrounding yourself with productive people?

Are you making an effort?

10

No Stopping Us Now

Now that we know that it is the spirit of the sloth that has caused us to act in laziness and procrastination, we must boldly speak deliverance. We are declaring and decreeing that there is *NO STOPPING US NOW*. We are producers and receivers of the promises of God.

Our minds should be made up that we will not give place to the spirit of the sloth in any way. We are willing and motivated to carry out tasks that we have been assigned and entrusted with. We are on our way into a higher dimension with God and should be giving Him praise for this right now.

We know now that God requires us to be productive *(They sow fields and plants vineyards, and get a fruitful yield. Psalm 107:37).* Thank God for exposing the evil spirit of the sloth. The Lord allowed us to see that this spirit caused us to mishandled our priorities, waste time, and to live a life-style of procrastination and idleness.

We must not forget that the spirit of slothfulness hinders the principles and powers of priorities. Our life is the sum total of all decisions we make. While it is true that God grants us free will and our decisions are ours to make. We as believers should live according to His will. As established in His Word, is not His will that we are slothful. We should seek His will even in all of our decisions and in all of our ways. It is written: *In All thy ways acknowledge Him, and he shall direct thy paths. Proverbs 3:6* . One of the greatest mistakes in life is being lazy and not allowing ourselves to acknowledge God. Being lazy and not acknowledging God can cause serious consequences. Let us look at the Word: *(Romans 1:28 ESV) And since they did not see fit to acknowledge God, God gave them up to a debased mind to do what ought not to be done.* We are going to be mindful, focus and keep pressing to put first things first *(No Stopping Us Now).*

We will no longer allow the slothful spirit to consume our time. It is often said that time is the "currency of life". How we spend it determines the quality of our life. We become whatever we buy with our time. Our time is important to God. No more being lazy. We are going to use our time for intentional purposes. We will not abuse or waste our time. Laziness causes time to be unimportant and it makes us as God's children look as though we are unwise.

We will no longer spend our time talking about what we cannot do. We are going to be doers. Laziness makes us comfortable spending our time doing nothing. We must know that God gave us time to be used for His Glory and not to wasted or mishandled . If we allow the spirit of the sloth to control our time we will find ourselves doing unnecessary activities that are not productive or pleasing to God.

Am I saying that we should spend all of our time doing nothing for ourselves…. Or that we should have no "me time" or "family time"? *NO!* We all need rest and recreation; God created us to rest. *JESUS told His disciples, "Come with me by yourselves to a quiet place and get some rest" (Mark 6:31).* The problem arises when we are able to find lots of energy to do the things that we want to do, but do not seem to have the same energy when it comes to doing those things that God has purposed us to do for the building of His Kingdom. The slothful spirit tells us that it is okay to put God's purpose and His agenda on the backburner. However, Jesus reminds us that we should **"Seek first His kingdom and his righteousness"(Matthew 6:33).**

Now that we are aware of this slothful spirit we are going to ask God to help us schedule our time more wisely. We are going to rethink how we spend our time and we will make adjustments so we can fulfill our Kingdom assignments. We are going to the next dimension in Him. We are going to pray that God surrounds us with positive people who are not slothful and wasting time.

Apostle Paul corrected the Corinth for hanging around the wrong crowd. He told them: **"Do not be deceived: 'Evil company corrupts good habits. Awake to righteousness, and do not sin; for some do not have the knowledge of God. I speak this to your shame" (1 Corinthians 15:33-34).**

These Christians were spending time with people guided by wrong values and acting in wrong ways. We can be affected by the actions and behaviors of others. Paul said that it was shameful. The Bible also tells us to use our time wisely and with great care. *"See then that you walk circumspectly, not as fools but as wise, redeeming the time, because the days are evil" (Ephesians 5:15-16).* We know that time is valuable and time is life and we will not waste it *(No Stopping Us Now).*

Procrastination will not be stopping us. We know what to do and when to do it. We are not just going to make attempts to start assignments, we are going to complete them. The devil knows that procrastinating is a trap that many of us fall into easily. We will not give in to this spirit because we *know now* that it carries severe consequences. It causes lack of productivity, it causes us to miss out on goals and it can make us feel that we are failures. Nevertheless, the Word lets us know that even if we do fall, we can get up and repent. Repent and keep moving. *(The righteous may fall seven times but still get up, but the wicked will stumble into trouble. Proverbs 24:16).* We will set goals and deadlines and press until we finish our tasks. We will not be held back by procrastination. *Philippians 3:14 EVS, I press on toward the goal for the prize of the upward call of God in Christ JESUS.* The scripture is encouraging us to stay focused on our goals. Focusing will help to prevent distraction and stumbling. *(No Stopping Us Now).*

Procrastination, laziness, and idleness are all birthed from the slothful spirit. Idleness, which starts in our minds, leads to stagnation. The spirit of the sloth will overshadow our minds and leave us in a state of wondering, thinking about whatever we wished, reliving and re-experiencing past images and memories, pondering and meditating on unnecessary things.

Thank God that we know now that an idle mind is an undisciplined mind and the thoughts of our mind controls our actions. We will not be slothful and idle. We will meditate on the Word. We will be alive, thriving, strong, and mighty. We will take our thoughts captive and replace them with the rich and powerful word of God. We know that idleness is our enemy. Idleness implies that there is nothing needing to be done. However look around at our young people, our ministries, the evilness in the world, all the people who are lost without Christ and even our own families… there is always something that needs to be done. We should not be idle because we know that is not what *JESUS* requires. *He told us, "As long as it is day, we must do the works of him who send me. Night is coming, when no one can work" (John 9:4)*

The Bible teaches us not to be idle but to be *"always abounding in the work of the Lord, because you know that your labor in the Lord is not in vain"(1 Corinthians 15:58).* We are going to be workers. JESUS said, " *The harvest is plentiful, but the workers are few. Ask the Lord of the harvest, therefore, to send out workers into his harvest' (Luke 10:2).* We know the value of being busy and not being idle. We will not spend our time day-dreaming instead we will seek the Lord for ways to make things happen. *(No Stopping Us Now)*

Excuses will not be an issue for us. We found out that the spirit of the sloth promotes excuses. We have allowed this spirit to keep us from being fruitful . We have become good at making excuses. As a matter of fact, we have become better at making excuses than we are at finding Godly solutions. It is always "someone else should do it", or "I don't understand", or "I don't have the finances", or "I don't have the time". However, the truth is that we just do not want to… because we are too lazy to trust God to see us through the task.

An example of how God viewed excuses in the Bible is one referencing the Prophet Jeremiah *(Jeremiah 1:6-9)* *Then said I, Ah, Lord GOD! behold, I cannot speak: for I am a child.*

7 But the LORD said unto me, Say not, I am a child: for thou shalt go to all that I shall send thee, and whatsoever I command thee thou shalt speak.

8 Be not afraid of their faces: for I am with thee to deliver thee, saith the LORD.

9 Then the LORD put forth his hand, and touched my mouth. And the LORD said unto me, Behold, I have put my words in thy mouth.

His excuse was that he could not or should not speak because he was young *(vs.1)*. I want you to notice *(vs. 9)*. God has a way for us to overcome our weaknesses and our insufficiencies. As one of my ministry colleagues would say, *"His strength is made perfect in our weakness . His Glory is manifested through our flaw."* We do not have to make excuses when we have the promises of God's provision. The Word of God adds that *(vs .9) Then the LORD put forth his hand, and touched my mouth. And the LORD said unto me, Behold, I have put my words in thy mouth. (My God, My God what a Mighty God we served).* We do not have to allow excuses to hinder us anymore. We can go wherever He sends us and speak whatever He tell us and we do not have to be afraid of anyone. He will deliver us. We are speaking in the atmosphere that there will be no more excuses.

(No Stopping Us Now)

We are going to stand with God. It does not matter how things look, how things smell, how things taste and what you hear. If we stand with God we will have victory. As we walk in our victory, being free from the spirit of the sloth, I want us to say boldly; *".Ain't nobody mad but the devil."* And if you would add this to it: *"And I like it like that."*

Now that the spirit of the *sloth* and others spirits such as:

procrastination, idleness, time wasters, laziness, inactivity,

excessive sleep, excuses, slothfulness and unwillingness has

been exposed, we can move forward to our next dimension with

God. *No Stopping us Now*! We are battle ready to take our

authority, legal rights and power back from the devil. Because of

being slothful we as born again believers have forgotten that we have

the power and the authority over all unclean spirits. We are about to

walk in to Kingdom territory. Our inherited territory… because we

are children of *The King*.

Because our minds have been freed from the spirit of the sloth,

doors that were closed in our faces are about to be opened and

blessings are going to be released. The power of God is going to

burst the enemy's bubble because now that we know our rights, we

will not be too lazy to ask God for what we want and we will not be

too lazy to press forward to get it. We have the right to "ASK "A=

ask, S= seek and K= knock. The bible tells us (*Matthew 7:7-8*)

Ask, and it shall be given you; seek, and ye shall find; knock,

and it shall be opened unto you:

8 For every one that asketh receiveth; and he that seeketh findeth; and to him that knocketh it shall be opened.

God wants us to ask Him for what we need and He will give it to us. And the Word tells us *(John 14:13) And whatsoever ye shall ask in my name, that will I do, that the Father may be glorified in the Son.*

14 If ye shall ask any thing in my name, I will do it.

Now that our minds are clear from the sluggishness of the sloth we should be preparing ourselves for greater. It is now time that we stop the silence, open our mouths and declare how we as people of God want things to be in our neighborhoods, homes, schools, churches and in our lives. God has already given us the authority to have what we seek. According to Matthew, *(Matthew 18:18) I tell you the truth, whatever you bind on earth will be bind in heaven, and whatever you loose on earth will be loosed in heaven.*

On this earth *Jesus* has given us the authority. We cannot be lazy in using our weapons. He will back us up. What we prohibit on earth, heaven will prohibit, and what we permit on earth, heaven will permit. In other words we have the say so and the power whatever we disallow, Heaven will make sure it does not happen.

It is time for us to spend our time making a change in the world. It is time for us to produce. It is time for us to have more than enough. The domain of earth is our legal right. The authority and power was transferred to us from the beginning of creation. It is written in the Word. *(Genesis 1:26) And God said, Let us make man in our image, after our likeness: and let them have dominion over the fish of the sea, and over the fowl of the air, and over the cattle, and over all the earth, and over every creeping thing that creepeth upon the earth.* **The KING** said I want to trust them " *The King's Children"* with the authority and power for earth.

The enemy wants us to sit back be idle-minded and believe that we have no say so over earth's territory. However, when God created mankind, he put the earth under human authority. The Bible reminds us:

(Psalms 8:6-8) Thou madest him to have dominion over the

works of thy hands; thou hast put all things under his feet:

7 All sheep and oxen, yea, and the beasts of the field;

8 The fowl of the air, and the fish of the sea, and whatsoever

passeth through the paths of the seas.

We are the people that have the authority and power to make an impact in this evil world. And when we speak God hears us. Let us look at **11Chronicles 7: 12-14**, the Lord said to Solomon "I have heard you and if I do decide to shut up heaven and cause some things to happen, they will happen… but if *" my people which are called by my name"* do something (loose) I will loose heaven. *2 Chronicles 7:12 -14 And the LORD appeared to Solomon by night, and said unto him, I have heard thy prayer, and have chosen this place to myself for an house of sacrifice.*

13 If I shut up heaven that there be no rain, or if I command the locusts to devour the land, or if I send pestilence among my people;

14 If my people, which are called by my name, shall humble themselves, and pray, and seek my face, and turn from their wicked ways; then will I hear from heaven, and will forgive their

sin, and will heal their land. It is time now that we start executing our authority so we can experience more of the supernatural from God.

God is waiting to expand our territories. Now is the time to prepare for Kingdom expansion. We are people with words of power and when we speak to God something happens. We will look back at II Chronicles 7 chapter again. If we notice the first verse: ***(2 Chronicles 7:1) Now when Solomon had made an end of praying, the fire came down from heaven, and consumed the burnt offering and the sacrifices; and the glory of the LORD filled the house.*** The Bible lets us now that when Solomon finished talking to God, opening his mouth, then something happened. Fire came down from Heaven. We have been given power in our words and with this power we can shake Heaven. And when heaven is shaken ***The Glory*** of the Lord will fill our houses. It is time that we pray and do not play. I believe that God is ready to release some abundant blessings to us.

We must pray more. We cannot be afraid to go back to our "prayer closet", as our older mothers would say. When we see the supernatural movement of God it will move us in to worship and praise. *(Verse 3)* *And when all the children of Israel saw how the fire came down, and the glory of the LORD upon the house, they bowed themselves with their faces to the ground upon the pavement, and worshipped, and praised the LORD, saying, For he is good; for his mercy endureth forever.*

As we keep reading the Word, we see that the people continued doing… they were not idle. They offered sacrifice verses 4- 5. *Then the king and all the people offered sacrifices before the LORD. 5 And king Solomon offered a sacrifice of twenty and two thousand oxen, and an hundred and twenty thousand sheep: so the king and all the people dedicated the house of God.*

As we see in verse 11, there was no procrastinating because the Bible says that Solomon finished the house. *Vs.11 Thus Solomon finished the house of the LORD, and the king's house: and all that came into Solomon's heart to make in the house of the LORD, and in his own house, he prosperously effected.* The

Word lets us know at the end of this verse that prosperity was the result of being a doer, staying focused and putting God first.

In this season, we must stay focused and hold on to faith. We cannot be distracted by our circumstances. I am encouraging you to hold on because if you do, there is going to be an unusual move of God in your life. Blessings are going to find you, health is going to be restored to you, wealth is going to come down to you.

We will not be lazy. We are going to do our part as the King's children. We are going to be motivated and put the work behind our faith. As I stated in a previous chapter, **"faith wants a job"** it is not asking us for a 15 minute break nor for a two week vacation. Faith will get the production out. Faith is one of the greatest weapons that we can use against the spirit of the sloth.

Our enemy, Satan is out to destroy the faith that we are holding on to. The more we hold on, the more he is coming with his attacks against us. Faith is a threat to the enemy and that is one reason we cannot sit around being idle. We have to work our faith. The enemy knows that by faith souls are saved, bodies are healed, weak become strong and the promises of God are received.

The Apostle Paul warned Timothy that in times of trials, some would cast aside their faith and Satan would use it to his advantage to destroy them.

(1 Timothy 1:19) Holding faith, and a good conscience; which some having put away concerning faith have made shipwreck: the enemy's goal is to get us to fail in our faith so that he can shipwreck us. Remember Peter came under a faith attack and *Jesus* told him that Satan hath desired to sift him to see if he would stand but the most important things not to let his faith fail. *Luke 22:31-32 And the Lord said, Simon, Simon, behold,*

Satan hath desired to have you, that he may sift you as wheat: 32 But

I have prayed for thee, that thy faith fail not: and when thou art converted, strengthen thy brethren.

We have to be watchful and alert of the spirit of the sloth. We have to hold on to faith through good and bad times. Paul encouraged us that no matter what he kept the faith. *2 Timothy 4:7 I have fought a good fight, I have finished my course, I have kept the faith:* Paul is saying to us, that although the enemy attacks, we still fight, and do not run out of faith. Paul encountered many attacks. Here are a few: Satan sends messengers to fight him in Jerusalem, Damascus, Asia, Ephesus, Antioch, Corinth. However, he kept the faith. He was shipwrecked, five times the Jews beat him with thirty-nine stripes, he was cast into prison, three times he was beaten with a rod and stoned and left for dead. He kept the faith. Paul added: *2 Corinthians 4:8-9 We are troubled on every side, yet not distressed; we are perplexed, but not in despair;*

9 Persecuted, but not forsaken; cast down, but not destroyed; yet he stayed focused and kept the faith and he didn't give up trusting God.

Now, after all the things that God has revealed to us in this book concerning the spirit of the sloth and its associated spirits that deter us from our God-give assignments, and ultimately keeps us from reaching our full potential of God's promises, are we ready to step up and put forth effort and energy to perform the tasks that have been given to us? Remember Chapter 1 of this book: *Matthew 25:15*

And unto one he gave five talents, to another two, and to another one; to every man according to his several ability; and straightway took his journey. We noticed that each were given tasks *according to his abilities.* So whatever task is given to us, God knows our abilities and He expects the tasks to be done. There is no more room for excuses, procrastination, wasting time or fear. The Lord is giving us a command to "*go.*"

We must be willing to go and we must have a compelling desire to reach those who we have been purposed to reach. We must let go of our own excuses and be willing to do the work of the Lord even in the face of rejection. We must compel souls to come to Christ. In this scripture we will find that people render all kind of excuses: *Luke 14:16-23 Then said he unto him, A certain man made a great supper, and bade many:*

17 And sent his servant at supper time to say to them that were bidden, Come; for all things are now ready.

18 And they all with one consent began to make excuse. The first said unto him, I have bought a piece of ground, and I must needs go and see it: I pray thee have me excused.

19 And another said, I have bought five yoke of oxen, and I go to prove them: I pray thee have me excused.

20 And another said, I have married a wife, and therefore I cannot come.

21 So that servant came, and shewed his lord these things. Then the master of the house being angry said to his servant, Go out quickly into the streets and lanes of the city, and bring in hither the poor, and the maimed, and the halt, and the blind.

22 And the servant said, Lord, it is done as thou hast commanded, and yet there is room.

23 And the lord said unto the servant, Go out into the highways and hedges, and compel them to come in, that my house may be filled.

Evidently the lord of the house knew the servant's ability because he told him to "go" in the highways and hedges and compel. The servant did not have the spirit of the sloth because he moved out of his comfort zone and made no excuses to bring people in.

This is what *Jesus* is requiring of us as born again believers. He wants us to *go* witnessing for Him and our ability to witness shall be powered by the gift of the Holy Spirit. *Acts 1:8 But ye shall receive power, after that the Holy Ghost is come upon you: and ye shall be witnesses unto me both in Jerusalem, and in all Judaea, and in Samaria, and unto the uttermost part of the earth.*

We cannot allow the enemy to make us believe that we do not need the power of the Holy Spirit. In order to reach the world with the gospel and make a stand against the devil we must have the power of God. We must have courage and boldness. The enemy wants us to feel that witnessing is a stressful activity, that compelling souls to Christ is a road of opposition, so we sit and become idle to this work. The Holy Spirit will empower and enable us in the face of opposition to keep proclaiming the gospel of Jesus Christ.

We must not be slothful. Paul said we must trust Jesus' promise that the Spirit will empower His witnesses to endure suffering and convict the world of the truth that is in Jesus. This is why Paul asked people to pray that he may have boldness to speak *Ephesians 6:19 And for me, that utterance may be given unto me, that I may open my mouth boldly, to make known the mystery of the gospel.* Instead of feeling powerless and doing nothing, we should pray for boldness and speak up.

Satan is the evil foe we face. We cannot toy with him he is out to make sure that we will not produce. He wants us to fail. He wants us to quit. His main goal is to steal, kill and destroy. We cannot be slothful. We must press to stay wise and alert of who the devil really is.

The devil is a liar he twists God's word to bring doubt *(John 8:44)*, he is the adversary. He prowls around like a roaring lion seeking who can devour. He searches for the weak and idle-minded. *(1 Peter 5:8)* He disguises himself as an angel of light. He will make laziness look good and it will be enticing. *(11 Corinthians 11:14).* He is a tempter. He tempts us with laziness, procrastination and idleness. *(Matthew 4:3).* The devil will do whatever he can to stop us from being fruitful *(1 Thessalonians 2:18, Matthew 16:23)*

We must keep ourselves protected at all times from the tricks of the enemy. We do not have time to waste. So we must fight to be aware, and stay alert *(1 Peter 5:8)* Submit to God's authority. Resist him and he has to flee. *(James 4:7)* Believe that in Christ, we are set free from the slothful spirit. We have the mighty power of the Holy Spirit working within us, and we are more than conquerors through Christ. *(Romans 8:37)* We are to be wise we will dress for battle daily, pray, stay in the word, *(Ephesians 6:11) We are aware, more than ever that we are in battle with a strong spirit of the sloth. Thank God for reminding us that " for that our fight is not against flesh and blood , but against the rulers, against the authorities, against the powers of this dark world and against the spiritual forces of evil in the heavenly realm (Ephesians 6:12).*

"Greater is He who is in us, than he who is in the world" (1John 4:4)

ABOUT THE AUTHOR

Mae P. Gaffney is Spiritual Counselor, and Warfare Intercessor at Touch 4 Love Outreach Ministries. She is CEO of Mae P. Gaffney Enterprises, LLC. She is Revivalist, Conference Speaker, and founder of the I Am Better Than That Empowerment Movement which encourages women, men, boys and girls to overcome strongholds by reaching beyond their circumstances and discovering a relationship with Christ. She is also the visionary behind the Women of Oneness Christian Network, which is established to bring together like-minded Christian women in unity to up-build the Kingdom of God.

Made in United States
Troutdale, OR
05/13/2025